The Dreamcatcher

A grieving mother's journey towards joy

By Jennifer Curry Prasad

ISBN: 978-0-578-56119-6

DISCLAIMER

The following story is true. All the events described herein are for the sole purpose of telling the author's son's story. The author does not assume and hereby disclaims any liability to any party for any loss, damage, or disruption caused by errors or omissions, whether such errors or omissions result from negligence, accident, or any other cause.

This book is dedicated to all the parents whose children visit them in their dreams.

I also would like to show my endless appreciation for my husband, Suresh, my daughter, Shayna, and my stepson, Triston for holding a loving space around me during the emotional rollercoaster writing process so Nico and I could share our story in hopes that we will help others struggling through their grieving journeys.

TABLE OF CONTENTS

A Midsummer Night's Dream

I dreamed about you again last night, Nico. You've been coming to visit me in my dreams more than usual lately. And the dreams, they're just...so vivid. And they feel so real, that when I wake up, I struggle to believe at first, that they're only dreams. I keep wondering if you're trying to tell me something; I wish I knew. It's been such a long time since we last spoke, but there's still so much I have left to tell you. So many things I want to say.

So, I'm putting it all in writing--into beautiful words--like a song in my heart that I'm finally ready to release from the deepest place within me. Of course, I'm painfully aware that you won't be responding. I'm certainly not expecting an email reply, or a letter in my mailbox, or one of those long, drawn out texts that you used to send me all the time. All I ask of you is that you listen.

In last night's dream, you were a little boy again, playing happily in the pool, just like you used to do all those years ago. But, you remember what kind of helicopter mom I was, don't you? So, of course I panicked when I saw that you were in the pool alone, and I quickly rushed to your side. Under different circumstances, I might have been amused that even my subconscious mind matches my overprotective ways in real life. Anyway, I came running over to you, eager to get you out of the pool.

And that's when the change happened, that sudden shift that threw me off, when you quickly transformed from a little boy to your sixteen year old self; the way you looked the last time I saw you. But, your teenage self wasn't happy like the little boy in the beginning of my dream. Suddenly, you were paralyzed and drowning, as I struggled in vain to get you out of the water.

No matter what I did, I couldn't save you, Nico. As soon as I got your head and chest above the water, your legs started falling under. I frantically pulled your legs up, but then your head and chest fell below the water's surface. You were sinking, and there was nothing I could do about it. The shimmering blue water that bore the distinct smell of chlorine and sunscreen harbored so many fun-filled summer memories. But now, it just looked sinister.

It reminded me of that day four years ago when everything in our lives changed.

Not Saved By the Bell

Thinking back now, you know what's so crazy about that day, Nico? It started out so *normal.* That's how it felt at the time, anyway. You told me that you weren't feeling well, so I let you stay home from school. I knew you well enough to know that you weren't lying. Just like any kid, you had your share of transgressions, but deception was never your thing, was it, Nico?

But you hadn't been feeling well quite often back then. It sort of became our normal, so I wasn't concerned. If there were any alarm bells, they weren't ringing loudly enough for me to hear them. You didn't look any different than usual. It was nothing a day of rest at home couldn't fix, right?

When I look back now, I want to blame myself sometimes for not recognizing what was going on with my boy. You may have been a teenager on the cusp of adulthood, but you were still my baby, and you always will be. But that's a whole other story, isn't it? Wasn't I supposed to have some kind of sixth sense that should have nudged me? Was there anything I could have done differently? Would things have turned out another way if I'd taken that day off, too? I'll never know the answer to that.

Taking the day off wasn't really an option for me, though. My new boss wasn't particularly lenient or understanding, even though she did have a sick child of her own. But my boss wasn't really the issue here. The bank I worked for was going through a merger, and a blackout was in effect, allowing no one a single day off. Business was business, and who were anyone's children to interfere with that?

Looking back sort of makes me wonder if we have to be in a certain situation in order to truly understand. If I'd announced from the very outset that I had a chronically ill child and would need the occasional day off because I had no choice, would things have been any different? Or would I have merely lost my job, only to be replaced by someone with a lighter load of what society likes to refer to as "baggage?"

I try not to think about that now because we can't change the past, can we? I took off for work, leaving you with Triston, who by all accounts has always been an amazing stepbrother to you. I know that you're cringing at that very word as you read this because you and Triston were more like true blood brothers. But, I digress. Of course I do. It's much easier to cut this train of thought right here, before it goes off the rails. Before the nightmare begins. Before I'm forced onto that carousel that keeps spinning and never stops, no matter how much I beg and plead to step off and go back to the way things were.

But, there's no going back, is there? And just like that perpetually spinning carousel, the story continues because four years have passed and there's no denying that, no matter how much I'd like to.

My phone rang right at noon that day, like the angel of death buzzing in my ear. It was *that* call that every parent dreads.

"Mom, my body's starting to feel numb." You spoke the words calmly, a little too calmly, when you weigh the meaning of the words you spoke.

That was all you needed to say for me to get the message. I instructed Triston to take you straight to the emergency room. I was on my way to meet you there.

Something serious was unfolding here. I didn't quite want to believe it yet, but denial can only take a mother so far.

Now, there were many things wrong with this picture, and I think that maybe you have to be a parent to truly understand it. This wasn't the usual stuff that sends dutiful parents to the emergency room with their often screaming offspring in tow. There were no broken arms here, or a concussion, or even a horrific reaction to a bee sting. Not that those things aren't sufficiently serious, or worthy of attention because of course they are. But there was something much deeper brewing here; a sort of twisted, big black hole that you and I were both forced into against our will.

Miles To Go

I remember driving like a maniac; how could I not? The other cars were just a blur as I flew past them. The yellow light up ahead was taunting me, willing me to slow down and stop. It was a menace that I was determined to ignore, so I blew right through it. But I wasn't reckless, or drunk, or irresponsible. I was just a mother rushing to meet her child at the emergency room.

I don't know if you remember this, Nico, but I actually got there before you did. I recall standing in the hospital parking lot, watching Triston's car coming towards me, as if all of this were happening in slow motion. I heard myself breathe a sigh of relief just as soon as I saw you, but of course, you and I both know that I exhaled *way* too soon. I could feel the anxiety bubbling up inside me, but I tried really hard not to let it show. That alone took everything I had in me. I wanted to put on a brave front for you, so you wouldn't be scared. But let's get real for a moment--you weren't exactly a little boy anymore. I couldn't play that game with you any longer. You were feeling what was happening inside your body, and you knew just how bad things were better than I did. I didn't want to see it that way at the time; no mother does. I wanted to believe I could protect you from everything. I had to try, anyway...what mother could do less?

I don't think I even waited for the car to come to a complete stop. I just remember rushing to your side and yanking the car door open with so much force, that I'm still surprised it didn't break apart at its hinges. My adrenaline had gone into overdrive and my emotions were already there to meet it, but somehow, I had to get through this. *We* had to get through this.

"Come on, Honey, let's go," I said to you, urging you out of the car so the doctors inside--you know, those people whom we consider demi-gods, as we hold out hope that they can pull off a miracle the same way a magician pulls a rabbit out of a hat-- could heal you. And then I'd take you home.

Home. That was all I could think about. I wanted them to fix my baby so that I could get him home. If only it had been that simple, Nico.

The problem was, when I opened the door and tried to usher you out of the car, you didn't instinctively step out the way you always did. Instead, you just sat there and stared at me. Just when I thought things couldn't get any worse, you finally spoke.

"Mom, I can't walk!"

It took a moment for your words to register. But only a moment. It wasn't just that you couldn't walk, as if that weren't horrifying enough. You weren't even able to get yourself out of the car. You couldn't move.

What in the world was happening here? My sixteen year old son, my little boy, the one who spent five to six hours a day playing basketball couldn't move to get out of the car. And that's when I knew we were in serious trouble. My nightmare was only beginning, though. Little did I know then that I still had miles to go.

Try Not To Blink

Sometimes, when I think back on that day, Nico, I try to imagine it from your perspective. It was the worst day of my life, but I don't want to forget a single detail. Trying to see it through your eyes has a way of forcing me to conjure up details that may have seemed insignificant at the time. Of course, you remember what happened next.

I remember running inside the hospital to get help. Well, that's the part you could easily see, anyway. There was a whole other battle going on inside me, though. I was trying really hard to fight back the horrific realization that was descending on me like a menacing black cloud. Watching the medical staff load you into a wheelchair and call a stroke alert had a sickening, surreal feel to it, as if I were in a dream and I couldn't wake up.

But, what must it have felt like for you, as you sat in the car helplessly, unable to perform the simple task of stepping out onto the pavement? What could you have been thinking when a crew of strangers came swarming at you, to lift you out of the car and place you into a wheelchair? Did you think about the hours of basketball you played just the night before, without any limitations at all? I have to admit, it seemed so bizarre to me. You were just fine yesterday. But that was yesterday. It's frightening how quickly everything can change.

Before I could even blink, they had you in a room, surrounded by at least 100 people. You know as well as I do that that's no exaggeration. There were literally 100 or more people surrounding you at that moment. That's what it felt like, anyway. I was hardly in a position to count. I was struggling to hold myself together. Of course, the real battle was just beginning.

There wasn't a medical test that they didn't give you, was there? The one that stands out the most to me was your CT scan, mainly because that's where the really bad news started. And then it just fell into a cascading set of dominos from there.

The only thing that gave me some tiny bit of comfort was how alert you were, Nico. Looking back now, it's disturbing to me to know that you were so fully aware of all the horrors that were going on around you. Disturbing is truly a rather soft way to put it, Nico. It tears me up inside, like someone ripping into the core of my soul to realize how you knew all along, that we'd reached a treacherous turn in our journey together. I wonder sometimes, did I seem calm to you? Was I a source of comfort? Or could you sense my unease as a feeling of dread that I couldn't quite shake enveloped me in a grotesque and unwanted hug?

The reason I'm asking is that at first you were your usual self, in spite of everything. That's saying a lot, actually, considering that you couldn't move your body at all. And let's be honest, here--that would potentially send anyone into a spiral of panic and chaos.

But then, your whole demeanor changed. I watched in horror as your calm face gave way to sobs and a mask of fear that I couldn't deny was entirely justified given the circumstances. You knew, didn't you, Nico?

I watched as tears ran down your face like sorrows that I couldn't fix. The most powerful way to torture a mother is to force her to watch her child suffer, especially if she knows that there's nothing she can do about it. I would have traded places with you in a heartbeat, if only such a thing were possible.

As I stood there helplessly, in a freezing cold hospital room with harsh fluorescent lighting glaring down on my terrified, crying son, I found myself thinking back to a much simpler time. It wasn't so much out of escapism because motherhood doesn't allow for that when your child is sobbing and immobile in the emergency room. It was more about watching my life flash before my eyes as I stood shakily on an unknown precipice, trying desperately to find some solid footing.

Two Lines On a Stick

I know you'll never understand this, Nico, but there's something that happens when you become a mother. It has a way of changing who you are. Your heart no longer resides inside your body. Your soul is not yours anymore; it's attached to someone else's soul. And the worst part is that you have no control. The craziest thing is that you often forget that there was a time in your life when you weren't a mother, before a perfect little person was entrusted in your care. Before you asked yourself what you did to deserve him. Before you knew you could walk on hot coals, or swim through the choppiest waters, or waltz right into a den of wolves if that's what it took to make everything okay for your child. There's a part of you that can't be whole just by yourself, because that person you brought into this world is forever an extension of you.

In that moment, when you're rushing your child to the emergency room, and you know it's not just a twisted ankle, you ask yourself how in the world you got here. How did it come to this? Why is this happening to me? And more importantly, why is *my* child being put through this?

My journey into motherhood didn't come simply or easily, but that seemed to be a common theme in my life, starting from the day I was born, or even before that, really.

I think back on that day that seemingly started just like any other day for you at the ripe but still innocent age of sixteen, and I realize with a bit of shock that by the time my mom was that age, she was already a mother herself. You know the story, Nico, for the most part anyway, so you know that I didn't exactly get the most solid start in life. But Grandma's always had a fighting spirit, so at least I know where I got mine from.

Some people may have looked down on my mother, since she was a teen mom who made two children with an abusive addict of a man. But there's something to be said about the wisdom of youth, too. Especially when that youth is a mama bear with cubs to protect. My mom took me and my brother, and walked out on my dad, fleeing the state altogether so that we'd be far enough out of his reach. We lived in a trailer behind a casino in South Florida, where my mom had to collect glass bottles and cash them in just to pay for my baby formula.

And the hospital where you were taken that day four years ago, Nico, was like a home away from home for me because I'd spent a lot of time there as a very sick child. You want to know what's ironic, Nico? That hospital you couldn't walk into that day was the very same hospital where I'd taken my first steps as a baby. I also remember my mom being skinny when I was a child. What I didn't realize at the time was that she was so thin because she didn't eat. There was never enough money to feed both herself and the kids. This may have seemed odd to me before you were born, Nico, but it seems very natural now. I also remember that my brother and I never knew what hunger felt like.

I was one of those weird kids, the kind who preferred to play alone, mainly because I had a whole crew of imaginary friends to keep me company. They somehow always seemed more fun than the real kids in the neighborhood.

And then, I grew up, and I met your dad. I didn't realize it at the time; I couldn't have, really, but that was a hugely defining moment in my life, solely because it led me to you.

Nico, I wish I could tell you that I was an angel who did no wrong back in my wild days of troubled youth. But that would make me a liar, and you know I have no tolerance for deception; that's one thing that you and I have in common. Your dad had me at the perfect pickup line--he just came right up to me and told me that he wanted to go out with me, but he knew I'd never go out with a guy like him. I don't know why, but at the time, it seemed like a really sweet and loving thing to say. Maybe even a little romantic in my twisted mind. Your dad and I were made of raging hormones, with no inhibitions, and we were ever so sloppily drunk on youth. What I'm really trying to say is that we were foolish and didn't use birth control. There was never any talk about the future; we hardly even thought about it, really. We chose to live in the here and now, as if tomorrow would never come. But it did in the form of two faint lines on a pregnancy test.

To your dad's credit, he didn't take off. Doing the right thing was generally not a part of his agenda, but he decided that he wanted to marry me, so that's what we did. Looking back, it seems really ridiculous to think of our getting married as doing the right thing. It seemed like the logical thing to do at the time, though. Every tick of the clock had a way of reminding me that motherhood was staring me down, and doing it alone didn't really appeal to me.

This is not to say that I never loved your dad, Nico. He was that older man who seemed wise, and safe, and protective when we first met. But, even then, I knew that I wasn't getting married for the right reasons. At the time, it sure seemed like the best decision I could have made for you, though.

So, I arrived like a zombie to our wedding, feeling less like a bride, and more like a guest who didn't really want to be there, but made an appearance just to be polite. I was almost five months pregnant at the time, but you'd never know it because I wasn't showing yet.

Of course, that would change soon enough. I'll never forget that sonogram when they told me that I was having a boy. It was starting to feel real, even though I was terrified and had no idea what I was doing. I could barely take care of myself, let alone a child. But, once I heard your heartbeat, I knew it would be alright.

After 32 hours of labor, you went into distress, so they had to bring you into this world surgically. I didn't want to do it because I was sure you'd come when you were ready. But, they told me that they had to get you out in a hurry for your own good, so I agreed.

Thinking back now, the day you were born was the first time a doctor essentially forced me into surgery to try to save your life. But sadly, it wouldn't be the last.

A Star Is Born

You came into this world screaming, announcing your arrival to anyone who would listen. It might have been the only time I'd ever be happy to hear you scream. A surge of gratitude washed over me because I knew at that moment that you were okay. And all of a sudden, dozens of hours of painful labor were washed away like they were never there, just by someone placing a precious little boy in my arms.

I don't know if I ever told you this, Nico, but looking into your eyes for the first time terrified me. Not because there was anything wrong with you; you were absolutely perfect in every way. It's just that I was staring at you, and when you returned my gaze, all I could see was a wise, old soul, like an old man who'd spent thousands of years gathering all the wisdom of the world. You were just so omnipresent; so fully aware of everything around you, as if it weren't your first day on earth.

"Are you guys sure?" I didn't ask the question, but I really wanted to. Believe it or not, it really was my first thought when I looked at you. I was young and dumb, and I felt totally unworthy of this amazing little spirit. Maybe you were intended for someone else, someone wiser, someone who actually knew what she was doing?

But they assured me that you were all mine. It was like one of those moments in a dream, where you're about to wake up, but you want to stay asleep so that the euphoric feeling can linger a bit. I had no idea what I did to deserve you. I just fell so madly, deeply head over heels in love with you, feeling a sudden sense of purpose and fulfillment that I never knew existed. You know how they say that your cup runneth over? I didn't know what that meant until I held you in my arms.

We named you Nicolos after your dad's father Nicolo, and my grandpa Nicholas. Of course, you would always be Nico to me.

Out of the Darkness and Into the Light

I stood there, flicking the switch, willing the lights
to come on. But darkness hovered over me as I
cradled you in my arms. I went to turn on the
faucet, but nothing came out. The electricity was
shut off again. So was the water. That's what happens when bills don't get paid. Your dad and I tried
to make things work; we really did. It was kind of
hard to do when I had no working stove to cook
your food, and no running water to bathe you. You
of all people know that I've never been much of a
cynic, Nico, but the truth is that sometimes love is
really not enough. To be fair, your dad and I
weren't exactly in love to begin with, so maybe it's
a moot point. But If I could pass on one tiny
nugget of wisdom, I'd want to tell you that babies
don't save relationships. Whatever was wrong be-
comes amplified once a baby comes on the scene.

Of course, we didn't get pregnant on purpose, so
neither one of us ever placed the burden of healing

our relationship on you. It's just that when your dad announced his decision to marry me, back when you were still a dream growing inside me, some part of me already knew that it was a bad idea. But it's hard to see clearly under the haze of what we think of is love. This was especially true for me because all I ever wanted was for someone to love me. Other people assured me that everything would change once you were born. Everything did change, just not the way everyone expected it to. I'd lost my willingness to accept anything less than what you deserved. It wasn't about me anymore. Maybe I could have lived in a world where money to pay the bills was being diverted for various chemical vices. But I knew instinctively that you were worth so much more. You were just too precious.

It's funny how cycles continue, isn't it? I thought about my mother as I packed you up and ventured into the dark cavern of single motherhood with little more than hope, prayers, and you in my arms. I wasn't going to keep you away from your dad because I really hoped that he'd be a good father, even if he and I weren't meant to raise you together. And your dad really did try; I know he did. But we all have our own demons to slay, and some of us are more proficient slayers than others. It wasn't long before your dad got arrested and spent much of your childhood in and out of jail.

I don't know how much of the early years you re-member, Nico. I spent every waking moment ei-ther working, or with you. We moved into a one bedroom condo where you got the bedroom and I slept on a tiny bed in the dining room. It may not have seemed like much, but I was so proud of it because I was able to keep that roof over our heads all by myself. You always knew me as your moth-er, and you were still so young that you only saw the good. But the truth is that the world just viewed me as a statistic--the product of a teen mom, a high school dropout, and just overall, someone who was never expected to amount to much. No one in the world would have expected me to be able to raise a child on my own.

But even in those early days, where life was lived in between moments of my rushing to get you to school, or to get myself to work, or to pick you up at the end of the day so we could have dinner and then wake up tomorrow to do it all over again, I knew that you'd saved me. All the crazy things I did, all the partying seemed light years behind me now. Suddenly, I had an amazing little soul to raise. You were always the wise one, though, and I'm pretty sure you knew it, even when you were too little to understand.

Big Brother is Watching You

The years flew by; they always do. The truth is that time is rarely on our side. Money was tight, but I found ways to keep things interesting. As I look back, I can't honestly think of anything that you ever missed out on, other than living in a stable, two parent family. I'd have loved to have found a suitable father figure for you, but one of the greatest things about you was your capacity to only see the good, even when you weren't so little anymore. You never stopped loving your dad, even though you knew he struggled with addiction and was not exactly known for being stable. You always blew my mind, Nico, because you were able to do that one thing that most people can't seem to do--you would just focus on the good and put the rest aside, as if you were putting it away in a box and then storing it in some faraway closet that no one ever needed to open.

As you well know, two lines came back to haunt me again. I was certain that you'd be my only child. Finding out that you were soon to be a big brother left me sobbing as if I were about to lose something. It's not so much that I was averse to having another child. It's just that, as you know, I'm *that* mom who worries about everything. Seeing my heart walk around outside my body was one thing, but how was I going to split it in two pieces? And how was I going to keep track of my heart walking around in two different directions? The very thought left me frightened and uneasy.

Would I love her the way I love you? Was it even possible to love another person as much as I love you? And you were already twelve years old...how was I going to start this all over again? I didn't really know how you'd take it, since you'd grown so used to having me all to yourself. Was I being fair to you to make you share me after all these years?

I had no reason to worry. I'll never forget the moment you held Shayna for the first time. You were so proud, looking at her as if she were your own. I had a fleeting moment of thinking ahead into the future, and realizing what an amazing father you'll be someday. It was such a bittersweet feeling because on the one hand, I wanted to keep you young and innocent forever. But on the other, I was curious and eager to see the adult you'd grow into.

What surprised me even more was how much the two of you loved spending time together. I never expected a baby and a teenager to find any common ground. But, do you remember that time I came down with food poisoning? You were the one who took care of her when I became sick, and you did it without my even asking you to. You were the one who helped pack and unpack the car every time we went somewhere. You were the one who was there to console her every time she fell down as she was learning to walk.

You always had a way of looking out for her, and you were definitely her favorite person in the world. Single mom life wasn't easy, but the bond between the two of you had a way of making it feel like a dream. This wasn't how I imagined it, of course. I dreamed of becoming a soccer mom living behind a picket fence in a fairytale marriage somewhere. The crazy thing is that life rarely turns out the way we expected it to. But seeing you and Shayna together had a way of reminding me that life still turns out pretty awesome, even if it's a million miles away from what we envisioned back when we still believed in dreams and happily ever afters.

I sometimes watch that video I took of the two of you, a lifetime ago, when she was still crawling. That was yesterday, and eight years ago. You two were sitting, facing each other, rolling a ball back and forth across the floor. Shayna used to get so excited when you'd play that game with her. That ball would soon become a huge part of your life, wouldn't it, Nico?

Bad Blood

You lived and breathed to play basketball. It seemed like every free moment was spent on the court, wasn't it, Nico? You weren't nearly tall enough to be a basketball player, but you managed to make up for that in skill. I was intrigued watching you back then. You had this interesting combination of raw, natural talent, and a passion and drive that were so strong that you were determined to practice until you were so good that everyone took you seriously, even if they towered a foot or more above you.

So, maybe I never became that soccer mom in a fancy SUV with those cutesy family character stickers on the back. And while I finally married my prince and we made our way to the suburbs, there were still no picket fences to be found. But I found my happy place anyway, just by seeing how happy you were, logging countless hours on the basketball court, hanging out with your friends. I never had to be *that* mom who had to tear you away from screens or video games, not that you didn't love those. But, you were like one of those kids of my generation who was eager to play outside.

We'd created a family, and we'd fallen into a groove. Life was good. I had a happy teenager who rarely got into any kind of trouble, and a happy toddler. Now, here's where I should mention that Shayna is nothing like you, Nico. She's definitely not an old soul, and she doesn't have your sweet, gentle nature. She's a firecracker who came to shake things up. But somehow, the two of you cultivated the strongest of bonds, making all those worries I had when I found out I was pregnant with her seem so silly now. Rumor has it that we humans just worry too much about things that will never happen. But what happens if life takes us in the other direction? More specifically, what do we do if something that we never worried about happens, and what if that thing is our worst nightmare come to life?

It all started rather innocently, now that I think about it. I always knew that I was lucky because when you were really young and I was doing all of this on my own, you were always healthy. You almost never got sick, even when something was going around. Maybe that's what had me so blind-sided, since this was so far outside the way your body usually operated.

I couldn't help but notice the bruises. I'd have to have been blind not to see them. They seemed to cover your entire body like some kind of bizarre, unwanted canvas of demented tattoos. I brushed it off at first, figuring that you were just playing bas-ketball really hard. I mean, boys will be boys, right? A little rough play had to be the culprit here. That was much easier than entertaining any other possibility.

But a water ride had an odd, ironic way of raining on that fantasy I harbored, that there was nothing odd going on with you. I remember when you got off that ride, you were bruised everywhere. I think, back then, I may have stopped breathing for a moment. Or maybe two. You may remember this story, Nico, but my favorite Uncle Chuck died of leukemia. I was just a kid at the time, but what I recalled clearly is that his very first symptom was bruises. At some point, you can no longer ignore the obvious, even if learning the truth really scares you. So, I called a doctor. What else could I do?

Do you remember that doctor's appointment, Nico? I recall the doctor's exuberance and gumption, as he assured me that you looked great, so there was nothing to worry about. He took your blood just in case, but that was almost an afterthought. He was so certain that your blood work would come up normal, that he sent us home without even waiting for the results. The only thing missing was the lollipop you were supposed to get afterward.

That's where the party ended, though. And I realize looking back now, that this was the exact moment that I stepped onto that carousel that never stops. It wasn't long after we left the doctor's office that my phone rang. Turns out that you may have looked fine, but you really weren't. Your platelets were way off. We were advised to go straight to the emergency room right at that moment.

Immune thrombocytopenia, otherwise known as ITP. That was the new villain in town as far as we were concerned. Of course, back then it was called idiopathic thrombocytopenia, but it's the same ugly disease. A shiny new name won't change that. But basically, it's a platelet disorder. Your immune system was destroying your platelets, so your bone marrow was trying to compensate for it, creating a coping mechanism inside your body that was just a sinister, twisted sort of a hamster wheel. I had so many questions, but there were no good answers. No one knew why. No one knew how. No one knew exactly when. And no one knew how to make this go away so that we could all get back to our lives.

It's funny how, if you'd asked me the day before your diagnosis if anything was bothering me, I'd probably have had a small handful of complaints about day to day to life. But suddenly, they seemed so trivial. All I wanted was to go back to a world where those little things were my biggest problems. How on earth did you go from being such a healthy child to someone the medical world looked at with some odd combination of pity and compassion?

It was a loss of virginity of sorts because this was where our innocence ended. We unwittingly ventured out of a simple, unremarkable existence, only to walk right into a world of constant blood monitoring. As you know, Nico, I've always been a spiritual woman, but not a particularly religious one. Here I was, though, pleading for divine intervention all the time, in hopes that your platelet count would be in its proper range every time we had it tested. Looking back, it seems odd that my whole world was suddenly reduced to a number. That's what life was all about in those days--just praying for the right numbers.

Dribbles and Daggers

I'm thinking back and trying to pinpoint exactly when your love for basketball took over your life. You know as well as I do that basketball was an important part of your story. Your first big heartbreak didn't involve a girl. It came from your finding out that you didn't make the high school basketball team. You'd been a star player on your middle school team, so how did it come to this, you wondered? I remember even then, feeling completely crushed for you because I wanted so badly to protect you from the inevitable disappointments life has a way of tossing in our direction.

I could feel the depth of your despair. I also knew you'd reached a point where your ego had gotten too big, and you were expecting things that you no longer thought you had to earn. That chip on your shoulder was really weighing you down. It's crazy to think that in your sixteen years of life, that was the first time I was ever truly worried about you and the direction you were headed. Of course, I didn't think about it that way at the time. But, objects sure do look different when you're looking at them in the rearview mirror, don't they? I watched nervously as you put away your basketball shoes, and made your way into a world of darkness where nothing was ever your fault or your responsibility. And you found comfort in what I can only kindly describe as the wrong crowd.

But true love never really dies. It may falter at times, but ultimately, all it ever seeks is a second chance, so you and basketball were never that far apart. My heart happily skipped a few beats as I watched the light find its way back to your eyes. Your shoes starting showing signs of wear again. And the bounce of a dribbled ball once more became the soundtrack of your life.

And then the diagnosis descended upon you like a pile of bricks being rained down without mercy. Your first question was exactly as I expected-- would you still be able to play basketball? Luckily, that was permitted, provided your friends didn't play too rough with you.. It seemed like odd advice for a group of athletic teenage boys, but it was better than the alternative. Mind you, I know perfectly well that you'd have continued to play regardless because giving up basketball entirely was a bitter pill that you weren't prepared to swallow. Nor were any of us in a position to shove it down your throat.

You looked healthy and you seemed healthy, so it was easy to forget that you were living under the whims of an unrelenting disease. The elephant in the room was that we still needed to test your blood constantly, and we needed to consider treatment options because we'd been forced to learn the hard way that what you see is not always what you get. The doctors talked about surgically removing your spleen because apparently, that would take a huge burden off of your body. But it didn't come without risks. You refused to even consider that option, out of fear that it would be the end of your days on the basketball court. It probably would have been, too. I was reminded once again of your being such a wise, old soul. You knew back then that there are worse things than being dead. Living without pursuing your passions wasn't truly living to you. And besides, old soul notwithstanding, you were still a teenager, and they have a way of thinking they're immortal. What's a platelet disorder to stand in the way of that, right?

But remember, I'm *that* mom who always worries about everything, so watching you push yourself to the extreme just to make the basketball team became a bit alarming. I'll never forget your words when I mentioned that to you, Nico. Do you remember what you said to me back then?

"I just don't think I have enough time, Mom." You looked me in the eye as you spoke those words, your big brown eyes clouding over with a curtain of genuine concern.

"What do you mean?" I asked in earnest. I really had no idea what you were talking about, even though it all makes perfect sense now.

"I'm afraid I'm running out of time," you told me with an odd mix of uncertainty and gumption, as if you weren't entirely sure what you were trying to say, but you knew without a doubt that you were right to say it.

Just three weeks later, on what started out as an ordinary day, you came home from school, and made your usual trek to the basketball court across the street from our house. If there's one tiny thing that gives me the slightest bit of comfort as I look back, it's that you had your favorite meal for dinner that night. It was a proverbial last supper, I suppose. You and I stood together in the kitchen, chatting and kicking back green juice shots while you cooked shrimp teriyaki and rice. Who knew it would be our last time doing that?

"My arm feels funny," you said, your big eyes staring into mine as they always did when we spoke.

"What do you mean," I asked, feeling a little uneasy, but only a little. We'd become so comfortable in our new, uncomfortable reality that an odd feeling in your arm didn't strike me as alarming.

You didn't really have a clear explanation. You insisted that your arm didn't hurt, it just felt funny. Maybe you'd logged too many hours playing basketball. When I thought about how much time you spent dribbling a ball and then aiming it into a basket, it seemed logical that this could cause anyone's arms to feel funny. I pushed back that nagging feeling in my gut, not so much because I didn't want to act on it, but rather, because I had no idea what to do. You can't act on something if you don't know what the proper course of action is. Per the doctor's advice, we'd already put you through horrific in-hospital treatments that left you incapacitated in your bed for days afterward. On the surface, they seemed worth it because they worked. Your platelet count found its way to the normal range after that. But not for long, so we'd have to keep doing them.

Life isn't lived on the surface, though, is it, Nico? No, life is like a swimming pool--we're both terrified of the deep end, and mesmerized by it at the same time. Nothing exciting really happens in the shallow end, or on the surface, for that matter. When you dig deeper, you'll find that there's some dark, twisted cruelty in the simple irony that sometimes, we have to completely sacrifice our quality of life in order to live. Of course, in your case, I felt you were too young to have to go through that. But let's be honest here, you're my baby, so I would have thought that even if you were already geriatric. But watching you suffer in pain for days as a teenager was the sharpest kind of dagger being plunged over and over again, deep into my soul.

The next day would prove that none of this mattered. Because we'd be on that fateful trip to the emergency room, not knowing that the carousel we were riding was about to spin faster than we could ever hope to keep up.

One Final Cut

Garish hospital lighting and the beeping of monitors everywhere, not to mention the somber feel in the air have a way of keeping anyone's mind from straying too far from the calamity unfolding. Even if you want to block it out, you can't. It's just staring you down from every direction.

What I'm trying to say, Nico, is that my reverie could only take me away for so long. I was jolted back to the reality of what was happening all around us, what was happening to *you*. For just a moment, thinking back on all the struggles of my youth was a sort of survival tactic. It had a way of putting things into perspective because I realized that my lonely childhood, my failed marriage, and my struggles as a single mom on minimum wage were a dream compared to what was unfolding in that very moment.

When you're the patient, and your life is on the line, you're terrified, mostly due to fear of the unknown, which, in all fairness, is a basic human instinct that can't really be avoided, no matter how brave you are. When you're the mother of the patient, it's a whole new kind of terror, sort of like drowning in purgatory as your mind taunts you with all the horrific possibilities of the hell you're about to enter.

You'd always been my rock, Nico, and you knew it, didn't you? You were the calm one, the voice of reason, the one who always saw the good in everyone and everything. Watching you fall apart in front of me, your emotions finally getting the best of you, despite your best efforts to remain stoic will forever be one of the darkest moments of my life.

I put my fears aside just long enough to calm you down. I told you it was going to be okay, and you believed me because I'd never lied to you before. I have to say that I've looked back on the moment more times than I can count, and I still wonder if I did the right thing. It served the purpose because you quickly settled down again. But, it also made me a liar, didn't it, Nico? I'll be forever haunted by that simple, yet ugly reality.

What could I have done differently, though? Would things have been any better if I'd told you the truth? To be honest, I didn't even know how bad things were just yet. It didn't take long for all that to change, though. Once the neurologist showed up, he pulled me aside to tell me that they were going to remove parts of your skull and put them in a freezer.

Wait, what? Was he kidding? The doctor spoke emotionlessly, as if we were discussing a simple business transaction, instead of the taking apart of my baby's skull. The natural progression of a stroke is that it quickly leads to a swollen brain, and that's when the irreparable damage sets in. You were considered worthy by virtue of your age, Nico. It was presumed that you were still young and elastic enough to recover, so removing parts of your skull and putting them in a freezer as if they were some twisted kind of ice cream in order to relieve the pressure on your brain made perfect sense. Not to me, of course, but the doctor seemed to think the idea was brilliant. I couldn't help but wonder if he was a parent, and if he'd still love the idea just as much had it been his child occupying your hospital bed.

I was trying hard to wrap my mind around what he was telling me. But he insisted that they'd recently done the same procedure on a young cheerleader, and apparently, it worked like a charm for her. Presumably, after the surgery, she cheered her way out of that hospital.

Was this really happening? I was actually talking to someone about allowing my son's skull to be turned into some kind of puzzle where pieces that fit were taken apart and then eventually, hopefully, put back together again. It felt like a scene out of a horror movie where you'd become the unwitting star, Nico. What other options were there, I wanted to know. The answer came at me like a kick to the face. In a word, none. The best case scenario was that you'd be another success story, just like that cheerleader.

This wasn't even the worst part of it, though. The neurologist informed me that if we didn't get your platelet count up, you had no chance of surviving the surgery altogether. So, that carousel went around again, taking us right back to removing your spleen. Their theory was that if they could get that out, you'd be strong enough for skull removal surgery.

Exit neurologist, enter hematologist.

Now, there's something you have to realize, Nico. All of this was the stuff of nightmares under the best of circumstances, but when the clock is ticking and every minute counts, and you're a mother being forced to make these sorts of decisions on the fly, it takes on a whole new hellish dimension. The doctors looked at things differently than I did. To them, you were just another patient whom they needed to get out of a jam so that they could send you home in whatever condition, just as long as you were alive. But I had to think about what your life would look like once we got to that point.

The hematologist seemed to understand my natural hesitation to let them remove an organ from your body. It may not have been a vital organ, but I was pretty sure you were born with it for a reason. And you'd been so determined to keep all of your organs, so how could I not honor your wishes? Of course, with the pressure piling on, my choice as a mother was not enviable. At all.

So, the hematologist attempted various treatments to try to get your blood work under control, and he really believed they had a solid chance of success. The hours passed in a blur as they monitored you constantly, pushing bag after bag of platelets into your body. The trouble came with that very last bag, you remember, the one that gave you an allergic reaction. Just as I thought that the carousel couldn't spin any faster, I watched you break out in hives. It seems kind of silly, now that I look back, that hives would upset me considering how much worse everything else was. But it served as an ugly reminder that we just couldn't seem to catch a break anywhere. You weren't even be spared an allergic reaction in our quest to stabilize you. And to top it all off, it had to wait until the very last bag, like the punchline of a cruel joke.

That night was darker than usual. I stayed with you, but I didn't sleep. How could I? Time was not our friend at all, was it, Nico? Somewhere in the middle of that endless night, you and I got a most unwelcome visitor.

"Will you consent to the surgery or not?" The ICU doctor didn't bother with pleasantries, nor did he mince words. He glared at me smugly, making me feel like a negligent mother if I didn't agree to a surgery that you had previously told me that you did not want.

Something didn't feel right. They'd pumped your body with so many things that cutting you open didn't seem like a wise decision. But, the doctor's query wasn't really a question. It wasn't the question he was asking, anyway. What he was really asking me was if I cared enough about you to let them cut you open in some exploratory way as if you were a medical school experiment. And then they warned me that you'd be left with an ugly scar across your abdomen. Did they seriously think that I cared about scars at that moment? I just wanted to go back to how things were yesterday.

I signed the consent form in a sort of stupor. It felt like I'd fallen into an endless pit, desperate to grab on to something on my way down. I remember the surgeon showing up, a frail-looking old man, who bore an eerie resemblance to the grim reaper. Looking back, there were signs everywhere that this was a bad idea. The trouble was that no other options were offered. My hesitation to send you off for a splenectomy was not viewed as a mother's natural unease at having her child cut up without being given a moment's grace to absorb the idea.

Of course, once I caved, it was like a light switch had been flicked. Suddenly, preparations were underway, and I was shoved aside again, while a whole crew of strangers hovered around you, eager to take you to get cut open. I watched helplessly as they pushed your stretcher down the hallway towards the operating room. I begged them to stop for a moment so that we could say a prayer for you. And then, I made my way towards you so that I could give you one last kiss before surgery, to ask you if you're really okay with this surgery, and most of all, to tell you that I love you.

But, I never got to do that, Nico. Your vitals started dropping, so the medical team rushed you into surgery before I got a chance to get close enough to see you. I never got to say goodbye, Nico. I'll be forever haunted that I couldn't even be granted that one simple wish. That one final moment while you were still awake, while you could still look into my eyes, while you could still tell me that you loved me, too. Of course, I know you did; that's not the issue. But I was denied that final moment, and so were you.

Mom, Can I Stay?

Your surgery was actually a great success, Nico. I remember breathing a sigh of relief when that ancient relic of a surgeon came out to tell me how well you did. We got a bit of good news for a change. We'd spent our time in the waiting room praying for this moment. As you know, I was never a very religious woman, but that night I realized that many more prayers are being uttered in hospitals than in churches.

You had yet to wake up, so I had to wait to talk to you. It was kind of like being in the eye of the storm. Everything looked calm and peaceful, but that was just a mirage. In the blink of an eye, all those machines that were hooked up to you started sounding their alarms, a whole team of doctors filled up your room, and panic ensued. I was once again relegated to the sidelines, like some afterthought instead of the person who made you.

The ICU doctor, the same one who'd virtually forced me to consent to your surgery, told me that he didn't think you'd wake up. From that very same surgery.

Wait, what? Didn't the surgeon just tell me that everything was great?

I'm glad you slept through that next moment, Nico. Don't get me wrong, I'd have done anything to get you to wake up again. In spite of everything, my natural inclination was still to protect you, even though I was completely helpless in that moment.

I remember the doctor getting right in my face, and asking me if I understand what he was telling me. Yeah, I understood his words, but I refused to accept them. I just couldn't believe that somehow, we ended up here. That my journey through motherhood would make a pit stop here was unthinkable.

It felt like an eternity passed before morning came, bringing with it, a neurologist to check your reflexes. I can't quite find the words to describe the sinking feeling I had as I watched. You didn't react to anything. It was in that moment when it hit me. I'd tried so hard to be strong since we got to the hospital, but suddenly, all my strength left me. I don't think I ever felt myself falling. I just remember hitting the stone cold floor, sobbing, pleading for you, begging for someone to just give me back my baby. This had to be a dream, and I was very ready to wake up.

Looking back on that moment on that frigid hospital floor, I finally understand the true meaning of the words "rock bottom." That hard surface hits you before you manage to hit it. And you don't even feel any physical pain. Your emotions take over, and suddenly, nothing feels right, and nothing feels real.

It wasn't supposed to be like this. When you take your child to the emergency room, you expect the doctors to fix him up and send him home, good as new. What you don't expect is that your child will be transferred to a metal drawer in the hospital morgue. I realize that life wasn't meant to be fair. I didn't get the most solid start in life, and I had to claw my way onto every new rung of that proverbial ladder that we're always climbing from the day we're born.

But being the mother of a dead child is just unnatural. There should be a rule in life that children always outlive their parents, no exceptions. I stared at you, lying peacefully on that hospital bed, seemingly asleep as if you'd wake up any moment. You looked like an angel. So, I picked myself up off the floor. I had to. I had to remain strong for you. Some part of me still hoped for a miracle. You were the baby sent to me from heaven to save me. And here I was, unable to save you.

It breaks my heart that you'll never experience being a parent, Nico, especially since you would've been so good at it. But, the truth is that it's always a battle because we really have no control. Parents do what they can to protect their children, but sometimes, you can do everything right and still find yourself planning your child's funeral. I wasn't neglectful, I wasn't resentful that I became pregnant unexpectedly, and I certainly wasn't ungrateful for the beautiful son I was given. I did everything right, so how did things go so wrong?

When we're faced with tragedy, our natural inclination is to cling to our roots. I ended up calling in a shaman because my Cherokee heritage coursed proudly through every fiber of my being. You were still on life support, and I just wasn't ready to let you go. But, as usual, you showed up to save me, Nico.

"He's asking you if he can stay," the shaman told me.

You were ready to leave this earth, Nico, but just like the sweet boy you've always been, even in death, you requested my permission. I struggled to imagine how I'd go on without you, but who was I to deny you that?

We brought Shayna to see you one last time. Of course, she thought you were sleeping. I was a bit jealous of her innocence, and her total lack of realization of the gravity of this moment. She was showing you her new toy that she got, eagerly telling you all about it. Believe it or not, she still remembers that conversation she had with you; she just thinks that you slept right through it.

In honor of your love for basketball, we turned off your life support during the Miami Heat game. Everyone who loved you gathered around you in that sterile hospital room to send you off on the next part of your journey. I watched numbly as all of the tubes were removed from your body, cutting you off from the machines that were keeping you alive. And then I laid my head on your chest, and listened to your heartbeat, right up until the very last one.

The Dreamcatcher

Nothing can truly prepare you for motherhood. There are no books, no bits of stale advice, and no nuggets of wisdom that can really give you any sense of what's coming. Both of my children weren't planned, but they were fiercely wanted, and they're loved in a way that no words can truly illustrate. Once you reach that place, where a perfect little person is completely dependent on you just to get through the day, it really doesn't matter if you ever planned to become a mother, or if you were granted the privilege without even asking to be so blessed. As you well know, Nico, you and Shayna didn't come with a book of instructions. Motherhood means having to figure it out all by yourself. And no one gives you a trophy and tells you that you're doing a wonderful job.

So, you adjust. You come to expect mishaps throughout the day, and you learn to live with walking around with stained clothes because your baby spit up on you in public. But nothing in the world can prepare you to bury your own child.

One day, I was helping you overcome the great disappointment of not making your high school basketball team. Not long after that, I was planning your funeral. I remember waking up the day after I lost you, crawling out of bed, and sitting down on the floor in my bedroom. I just sat there for what felt like hours, staring at the floor. None of this felt real, yet I knew it was. I had to accept the loss of you. It's not that simple, though. Loss is not something clinical that we just absorb because it's true.

Every time I heard the front door open, I'd feel a jolt like it was you, coming home from playing basketball with your friends like you used to do. But that never happencd.

I wonder sometimes, if I'd have been able to get by without Shayna. I say this not so much because having another child meant that at least I wouldn't suddenly find myself childless. Any mother knows that no matter how many children you have, they never make up for the loss of a single one. It was having to take care of Shayna that got me through the first few days. Taking care of her served as a distraction to keep me from focusing on the stark reality that I had to face. I've come to realize, Nico, that simple distractions may be the one thing that keeps us sane when we're struggling to cope with the darker side of life. You always made sure your baby sister was taken care of. I knew that there was nothing better I could do for you than put what little energy I had left into her.

But if I'm going to be honest here, Nico, I have to admit that I was just going through the motions. I became a shell of a woman, more like a robot than anything else, just getting through the tasks necessary to keep myself and my other child alive. If I hadn't mentally checked out, I'd have found myself on the psych ward of that very same hospital. I like to think of it as living by proxy because I was still pulling all the levers, but no one was really home in my mind and in my heart. That vacancy served to keep me functioning at the most basic level, which was all I was capable of at the time. I found myself struggling against the desire to go to sleep and hope that I'd wake up to find that it was just a dream. Or at least go to sleep and not wake up at all. Don't get me wrong, I'd never failed to recognize the privilege of being alive. I was just adjusting to losing what I'd previously lived for.

I want to say that I've always had a life outside of being a mother. I was never one of those women who identified 100% as someone's mom and nothing else. But at the end of the day, being a mother means that you live for your children. I may not have realized that before I lost you, Nico, but I sure did understand it after you were gone. If someone had asked me before that fateful trip to the emergency room, I'd have said without hesitation that I can't live without you. Now I had to learn to go on being fully aware that I'd never see you again. Not in this lifetime, anyway.

One of my biggest sorrows is that Shayna has to grow up without you. She still remembers you, but barely. She was so young at the time that it's hard to expect any different from her. But, when I asked her what she wished people knew about you, she answered without a moment's hesitation. *That he had a little sister.* I wonder sometimes if you were the one who fed her that answer from The Other Side, solely because I know how important she's always been to you, ever since the day she was born.

There's so much more the world needs to know about you, though. I have so many great memories, Nico. I think back on the time I took you to meet Joel Osteen, and how easily you two hit it off, as if you were old friends. I remember the time I took you to the zoo and you were beaming because you got to hold a baby tiger. I remember how much you loved Jeff Dunham because he made you laugh. And most of all, there was your love for basketball, and your dreams of becoming a professional player someday. Taken alone, none of those things are particularly remarkable. But, when I think back on the book of your life, I have to smile, even though I'm smiling through tears because you were such an amazing human being.

How in the world was I so lucky to be your mother? The sixteen years I had with you were filled with enough joy to carry me through a thousand lifetimes. I've come to realize that in loss, we have to remember how blessed we were to have something we were so afraid of losing. I wonder all the time what I did to deserve you and Shayna. You've brought a whole new kind of meaning to my life that was never there before. How was I deemed worthy enough to be a mother, to bring a soul from one plane of existence into another, to soak up all the wisdom you sprinkled over my life for those sixteen years?

Your life was cut short, Nico, there's no question about that. But the truth is that a life, however short, is still a lifetime. You were and always will be my dream child. You came here for a short while, ephemeral when you think of how long your life truly should have been. But, you came here to change the world, and I'm determined to help you do that, even if you're only here in spirit to walk beside me.

So, I had no choice but to find joy in life again, Nico. I know I couldn't have done that without you. You never liked to see me unhappy. And, I'm not going to lie, it hasn't been an easy or seamless journey, and I still have my dark moments. Emotions come in waves, and since you loved the ocean so much, you know that every wave has a crest and a trough. Sometimes, I'm riding that wave, and life is good again. And other times, the struggle is as fresh as it was four years ago. But, I knew I owed it to you to enjoy my life. No amount of suffering on my part would ever bring you back.

I still recall the first time I laughed again. You remember my friend, Sara, don't you, Nico? She came over and did a silly dance, gyrating around like a crazy lady until the laughter came. The sound of myself laughing startled me at first, since it had been so long that I'd barely recognized the sound or the sensation. I remember loving the way it felt, while drowning in guilt at the same time. No matter how much I rationalized that you'd want me to be happy again, it still somehow seemed wrong at first. It felt so far away from that moment, just weeks prior at your funeral, when I stood over your casket, stared at you, and willed you to wake up and tell me that this was all a prank.

The wildest thing is that as soon as I made a decision to become happy again, you started sending me signs. From the text, addressed to you, I got from a random stranger seeking medical results, to your favorite songs randomly coming on the radio, to hearing your name paged at the airport. I'm fully aware, Nico, that you've orchestrated everything in my life since the day you moved your journey to another dimension, so I had to write this to you, just to make sure you understood how grateful I am to be able to call you my son.

So, let's talk about that dream some more, Nico. At first, it felt like another reminder that I'd failed you. But then, the rest of the dream flashed before me. It's not that I hadn't remembered it in the first place. It's just that as a mother, my initial focus was on my total inability to save you.

"I'm not that little boy anymore," you said to me, as you started floating away.

"Are you saying that this is how your life would be had you stayed?" I asked you, trying hard to understand what you were telling me.

You nodded with gumption, almost as if the answer was so obvious that I should feel a bit silly for even asking such a question.

So, that's the reality, isn't it, Nico? Had you survived that surgery, and presumably, survived the next one where they'd take your skull apart and store parts of it in a freezer, you'd have returned with nothing to live for. Your body would no longer be fit for basketball, or much of anything, really, would it? The shell of a person that I was as I came to grips with losing you is exactly what you'd have been relegated to for the rest of your life. You'd be alive, but your body would be your prison.

I get it, Nico, there are worse things than being dead. But life with you, even if you're only with me in spirit these days, is definitely worth living. So, I've come to realize that life truly is a gift, and we're lucky to be here. You never really left; you're just here in a different form. You remind me all the time that you're still beside me in everything I do. I've come to realize, Nico, that this is the message you wanted to say to the world, and that the only way you could make it known is by taking your journey to The Other Side.

The truth is that we never really lose anyone. We lose them in the physical form, but just because we can't see them doesn't mean they stop existing. Energy is never destroyed; it merely changes form. And love, especially the pure, unbridled love between a mother and child never dies. It's like a chain that can't be broken. It flourishes in a whole new, deeper way, from soul to soul, instead of person to person.

That's not to say that I don't miss seeing you, Nico. So, we need to come to an agreement. The only way I get to see you these days is in my dreams. And life is ultimately a series of dreams we're all trying to catch and hold on to. So, I bought a new dreamcatcher that I'm putting on my bedroom window just for you. It's got a tree in the middle of the circle, just like the tree of life that brought you to me as a perfect little bundle of wisdom and consciousness. And no dreamcatcher would be complete without a plume of feathers hovering under the circle.

So, think of it as an invitation, a request, an order of sorts because I'm still your mother. Come visit me in my dreams, Nico, so that I can see you, not that I'd ever forget what you look like. You've always been a healer in my world. This is our moment to heal the world together.

#And1ForMyAngelNico

Afterward

I lost my son in 2015 at the age of sixteen. He'd have been twenty years old this year. I wonder often what he'd be doing now had he survived, but it wasn't meant to be. As a parent of a deceased child, I've come to find that there are many of us out there, and the struggle of figuring out how to find joy in our lives is a lifetime struggle. But it's a struggle that we can win, and more importantly, it's a struggle we were meant to overcome. The greatest thing I can do for Nico is spread his love for life and his constantly happy demeanor to the world.

Now you know my story, and I'd love to hear yours. Most of all, I want to tell you that there absolutely *is* life after loss, and you can live your best life, no matter how dark your past has been, and how much trauma you've had to suffer.

Jennifer@JenniferCurryPrasad.com

About the Author

Jennifer Curry Prasad is a recovering banker, holistic health practitioner, hair whisperer, mindset success coach, mother to an angel son and sassy sweet firecracker princess.

When her teenaged son suddenly became ill and passed away, Jennifer's world shattered in to a million pieces. This trauma lead her to walk away from a very successful corporate banking career that she spent 23 years building. She started to build a business more aligned with her soul and in a way that helps bring change to people's lives every day.

She is fully convinced that her son carefully nudged her on to this path one baby step at a time from The Other Side and she now spends her days building her magical empire, building a community for her business partners based on mindset and energy practices for confidence building so the people she leads can build their empires and experience success. You can find Jennifer traveling the world, hair whispering, Lighting the path for others to build a more freedom based lifestyle.

Made in the USA
Middletown, DE
05 January 2024

47258555R00044